The Path of Waiting

D1297488

HENRI J. M. NOUWEN

The Path of Waiting

CROSSROAD • NEW YORK

1995

The Crossroad Publishing Company
370 Lexington Avenue, New York, NY 10017

Copyright © 1995 by Henri J. M. Nouwen

Printed in the United States of America

ISBN 0-8245-2000-9

I WANT TO REFLECT ON SOMETHING that has been on my mind during the past few years. It is something I have come to believe is very important for our time: a spirituality of waiting. What does waiting mean in our lives?

In order to explore this question, I would like to look at two aspects of waiting. One is the waiting *for* God, and the other is the waiting *of* God. We are waiting. God is waiting. The first two chapters of Luke's Gospel set the context for my thoughts on the waiting for God. The final chapters of the same Gospel provide the framework for thinking about the waiting of God.

Tapes of this material are available from Ave Maria Press (Notre Dame, IN 46556) or your local religious bookstore.

The story of Jesus' birth introduces us to five people who are waiting — Zechariah and Elizabeth, Mary, Simeon, and Anna. The story of Jesus' death and resurrection reveals to us a God who is waiting.

Our Waiting for God

Waiting is not a very popular attitude. Waiting is not something that people think about with great sympathy. In fact, most people consider waiting a waste of time. Perhaps this is because the culture in which we live is basically saying, "Get going! Do something! Show you are able to make a difference! Don't just sit there and wait!" For many people, waiting is a dry desert

*The story of Jesus'
death and resurrection
reveals to us a God
who is waiting.*

between where they are and where they want to go. And people do not like such a place. They want to get out of it by doing something.

In our particular historical situation, waiting is even more difficult because we are so fearful. One of the most pervasive emotions in the atmosphere around us is fear. People are afraid — afraid of inner feelings, afraid of other people, and also afraid of the future. Fearful people have a hard time waiting, because when we are afraid we want to get away from where we are. But if we cannot flee, we may fight instead. Many of our destructive acts come from the fear that something harmful will be done to us. And if we take a broader perspective — that not only individuals but whole communities and nations might be afraid of being harmed — we can understand how hard it is to wait and how tempting it is to act. Here are the roots of a "first strike" approach to others. People who live in a world of fear are more likely to make aggressive, hostile, destructive responses than people who are not so frightened. The more afraid we are, the harder waiting becomes. That is why waiting is such an unpopular attitude for many people.

It impresses me, therefore, that all the figures who appear on the first pages of Luke's Gospel are waiting. Zechariah and Elizabeth are waiting. Mary is waiting. Simeon and Anna, who were there at the temple when

Jesus was brought in, are waiting. The whole opening scene of the good news is filled with waiting people. And right at the beginning all those people in some way or another hear the words, "Do not be afraid. I have something good to say to you." These indicate that Zechariah, Elizabeth, Mary, Simeon, and Anna are waiting for something new and good to happen to them.

Who are these figures? They are the representatives of waiting Israel. The Psalms are full of this waiting. "My soul is waiting for the Lord. I count on his word. My soul is longing for the Lord more than watchman for daybreak. Let the watchman count on daybreak and Israel on the Lord. Because with the Lord there is mercy, and fullness of redemption" (Ps. 129:5–7, GRAIL). "My soul is waiting for the Lord" — that is the theme that reverberates all through the Hebrew Scriptures.

But not all who dwell in Israel are waiting. In fact we might say that the prophets criticized the people (at least in part) for giving up their attentiveness to what was coming. Waiting finally became the attitude of the remnant of Israel, of that small group of Israelites that had remained faithful.

The prophet Zephaniah says, "In your midst I will leave a humble and lowly people, and those who are left in Israel will seek refuge in the name of Yahweh. They will do no wrong, will tell no lies; and the perjured tongue will no longer be found in their mouths" (Zeph. 3:12–13, JB). It is the purified remnant of faithful people who are waiting. Elizabeth, Zechariah, Mary, Simeon, and Anna are the representatives of that remnant. They have been able to wait, to be attentive, to live expectantly.

Now I would like to turn our attention to two things. First, what is the nature of waiting? And second, what is the practice of waiting? How are they waiting and how are we called to wait with them?

The Nature of Waiting

Waiting, as we see it in the people on the first pages of the Gospel, is waiting with a sense of promise. "Zechariah, your wife Elizabeth is to bear you a son." "Mary, listen! You are to conceive and bear a son" (Luke 1:13, 31, JB). People who wait have received a promise that allows them to wait. They have received something that is at work in them, like a seed that has started to grow. This is very important. We can really wait only if what we are waiting for has already begun for us. So waiting is never a movement from nothing to something. It is always a movement from something to something more. Zechariah, Elizabeth, Mary, Simeon, and Anna were living with a promise that nurtured them, that fed them, and that made them able to stay where they were. And in this way, the promise could realize itself within them and through them.

Secondly, waiting is active. Most of us think of waiting as something very passive, a hopeless state determined by events totally out of our hands. The bus is late? You cannot do anything about it, so you have to sit there and just wait. It is not difficult to understand the irritation people feel when somebody says, "Just wait." Words like that seem to push us into passivity.

But there is none of this passivity in Scripture. Those who are waiting are waiting very actively. They know that what they are waiting for is growing from the ground on which they are standing. That's the secret. The secret of waiting is the faith that the seed has been planted, that something has begun. Active waiting means to be present fully to the moment, in the conviction that something is happening where you are and that you want to be present to it. A waiting person is someone who is present to the moment, who believes that this moment is *the moment.*

A waiting person is a patient person. The word "patience" means the willingness to stay where we are and live the situation out to the full in the belief that something hidden there will manifest itself to us. Impatient people are always expecting the real thing to

*The secret of waiting
is the faith that the seed
has been planted,
that something
has begun.*

happen somewhere else and therefore want to go elsewhere. The moment is empty. But patient people dare to stay where they are. Patient living means to live actively in the present and wait there. Waiting, then, is not passive. It involves nurturing the moment, as a mother nurtures the child that is growing in her womb. Zechariah, Elizabeth, Mary, Simeon, and Anna were present to the moment. That is why they could hear the angel. They were alert, attentive to the voice that spoke to them and said, "Don't be afraid. Something is happening to you. Pay attention."

But there is more. Waiting is open-ended. Open-ended waiting is hard for us because we tend to wait for some-

thing very concrete, for something that we wish to have. Much of our waiting is filled with wishes: "I wish that I had a job. I wish the weather were better. I wish the pain would go." We are full of wishes, and our waiting easily gets entangled in those wishes. For this reason, a lot of our waiting is not open-ended. Instead, our waiting is a way of controlling the future. We want the future to go in a very specific direction, and if this does not happen we are disappointed and can even slip into despair. That is why we have such a hard time waiting; we want to do the things that will make the desired events take place. Here we can see how wishes tend to be connected with fears.

But Zechariah, Elizabeth, Mary, Simeon, and Anna were not filled with wishes. They were filled with hope. Hope is something very different. Hope is trusting that something will be fulfilled, but fulfilled according to the promises and not just according to our wishes. Therefore, hope is always open-ended.

I have found it very important in my own life to let go of my wishes and start hoping. It was only when I was willing to let go of wishes that something really new, something beyond my own expectations, could happen to me. Just imagine what Mary was actually saying in the words, "I am the handmaid of the Lord. Let what you have said be done to me" (Luke 1:38, JB). She was saying, "I don't know what this all means, but I trust that good things will happen." She trusted so deeply that her waiting was open to all possibilities. And she did not want to control them. She believed that when she listened carefully, she could trust what was going to happen.

To wait open-endedly is an enormously radical attitude toward life. It is trusting that something will happen to us that is far beyond our own imaginings. It is giving up control over our future and letting God define our life. It is living with the conviction that God

To wait open-endedly is an enormously radical attitude toward life.

molds us according to God's love and not according to our fear. The spiritual life is a life in which we wait, actively present to the moment, expecting that new things will happen to us, new things that are far beyond our own imagination or prediction. That, indeed, is a very radical stance toward life in a world preoccupied with control.

The Practice of Waiting

Now let me say something about the practice of waiting. How do we wait? We wait together, with God's word in our midst.

Waiting is first of all a waiting together. One of the most beautiful passages of Scripture is Luke 1:39–56, which tells us about Mary's visit to Elizabeth. What happened when Mary received the words of promise? She went to Elizabeth. Something was happening to Elizabeth as well as to Mary. But how could they live that out?

I find the meeting of these two women very moving, because Elizabeth and Mary came together and enabled each other to wait. Mary's visit made Elizabeth aware of what she was waiting for. The child leapt for joy in her. Mary affirmed Elizabeth's waiting. And then Elizabeth said to Mary, "Blessed is she who believed that the promise made her by the Lord would be fulfilled" (Luke 1:45, JB). And Mary responded, "My soul proclaims the greatness of the Lord" (Luke 1:46, JB). She burst into joy herself. These two women created space for each other to wait. They affirmed for each other that something was happening worth waiting for.

Here we see a model for the Christian community. It is a community of support, celebration, and affirmation in which we can lift up what has already begun in us. The visit of Elizabeth and Mary is one of the Bible's most beautiful expressions of what it means to form community, to be together, gathered around a promise, affirming what is happening among us.

That is what prayer is all about. It is coming together around the promise. That is what celebration is all about. It

*Christian community is
the place where we keep
the flame alive among us
and take it seriously,
so that it can grow and
become stronger in us.*

is lifting up what is already there. That is what Eucharist is about. It is saying "Thanks" for the seed that has been planted. It is saying "We are waiting for the Lord, who has already come."

The whole meaning of the Christian community lies in offering each other a space in which we wait for what we have already seen. Christian community is the place where we keep the flame alive among us and take it seriously, so that it can grow and become stronger in us. In this way we can live with courage, trusting that there is a spiritual power in us that allows us to live in this world without being seduced constantly by despair. That is how we dare to say that God is a God of love even when we see hatred all around us.

That is why we can claim that God is a God of life even when we see death and destruction and agony all around us. We say it together. We affirm it in each other. Waiting together, nurturing what has already begun, expecting its fulfillment — that is the meaning of marriage, friendship, community, and the Christian life.

In the second place, our waiting is always shaped by alertness to the word. It is waiting in the knowledge that someone wants to address us. The question is, are we home? Are we at our address, ready to respond to the doorbell? We need to wait together to keep each other at home spiritually, so that when the word comes it can become flesh in us. That is why the Book

27

of God is always in the midst of those who gather. We read the word so that the word can become flesh and have a whole new life in us.

Simone Weil, a Jewish writer, said, "Waiting patiently in expectation is the foundation of the spiritual life." When Jesus speaks about the end of time, he speaks precisely about the importance of waiting. He says that nations will fight against nations and that there will be wars and earthquakes and misery. People will be in agony and they will say, "The Christ is there! No, he is here!" Many will be confused, and many will be deceived. But Jesus says, you must stand ready, stay awake, stay tuned to the word of God, so that you will survive all that is going to happen and be able to stand confidently (*con-fide*, with trust) in the presence of God together in community (see Matt. 24). That is the attitude of waiting which allows us to be people who can live in a very chaotic world and survive spiritually.

God's Waiting for Us

In the passion and resurrection of Jesus we see God as a waiting God. That is the second aspect of waiting that affects our whole spiritual life. So it is to the end of Jesus' life that I want to turn our attention. Let me start with a story.

I was invited to visit a friend who was very sick. He was a man about fifty-three years old who had lived a very active, useful, faithful, creative life. Actually, he was a social activist who had cared deeply for people, especially the poor. When he was fifty he discovered that he was suffering from cancer. During the three years that followed he became increasingly disabled.

When I came to him, he said to me, "Henri, here I am lying in this bed, and I don't even know how to think about being sick. My whole way of thinking about myself is in terms of action, in terms of doing things for people. My life is valuable because I've been able to do many things for many people. And suddenly, here I am, passive, and I can't do anything anymore.... Help me to think about this situation in a new way. Help me to think about my not being able to do anything anymore so I won't be driven to despair. Help me to understand what it means that now all sorts of people are doing things to me over which I have no control."

As we talked I realized that he was constantly wondering, "How much can I still do?" Somehow my friend had learned to think about himself as a man who was worth what he was doing. And so when he got sick, his hope seemed to rest on the idea that he might get better and return to what he had been doing. I realized, too, that this way of thinking was hopeless because he had cancer and was going to get worse and worse. He would die soon. If the spirit of my friend was dependent on how much he would still be able to do, what did I have to say to him?

In the context of these thoughts we read together a book called *The Stature of Waiting* by British author V. H. Vanstone.* Vanstone writes about Jesus' agony in the Garden of Gethsemane and his way to the cross. I want to draw on this powerful book in what follows. It helped my friend and me to understand better what it means to move from action to passion.

---

*V. H. Vanstone, *The Stature of Waiting* (Winston-Seabury Press, 1983).

From Action to Passion

The central word in the story of Jesus' arrest is one I never thought much about. It is "to be handed over." That is what happened in Gethsemane. Jesus was handed over. Some translations say that Jesus was "betrayed," but the Greek says, "to be handed over." Judas handed Jesus over (see Mark 14:10). But the remarkable thing is that the same word is used not only for Judas but also for God. God did not spare Jesus, but handed him over to benefit us all (see Rom. 8:32).

So this term "to be handed over" plays a central role in the life of Jesus. Indeed, this drama of being handed over divides the life of Jesus radically in two. The first part of Jesus' life is filled with activity. Jesus takes all sorts of initiatives. He speaks; he preaches; he heals; he travels. But immediately after Jesus is handed over, he becomes the one to whom things are being done. He's being arrested; he's being led to the high priest; he's being taken before Pilate; he's being crowned with thorns; he's being nailed on a cross. Things are being done to him over which he has no control. That is the meaning of passion — being the recipient of other people's actions.

It is important for us to realize that when Jesus says, "It is accomplished" (John 19:30), he does not simply mean, "I have done all the things I wanted to do." He also means, "I have allowed things to be done to me that needed to be done to me in order for me to fulfill my vocation." Jesus does not fulfill his vocation in action only, but also in passion. He doesn't just fulfill his vocation by doing the things the Father sent him to do, but also by letting things be done to him that the Father allows to be done to him.

Passion is a kind of waiting — waiting for what other people are going to do. Jesus went to Jerusalem to announce the good news to the people of that city. And Jesus knew that he was going to put a choice before them: Will you be my disciple, or will you be my executioner? There is no middle ground here. Jesus went to Jerusalem to put people in a situation where they

35

Here we glimpse
the mystery of
God's incarnation.
God became human
not only to act among us
but also to be the recipient
of our responses.

had to say "Yes" or "No." That is the great drama of Jesus' passion: he had to wait upon how people were going to respond. What would they do? Betray him or follow him? In a way, his agony is not simply the agony of approaching death. It is also the agony of having to wait. It is the agony of a God who depends on us for how God is going to live out the divine presence among us. It is the agony of the God who, in a very mysterious way, allows us to decide how God will be God. Here we glimpse the mystery of God's incarnation. God became human not only to act among us but also to be the recipient of our responses.

All action ends in passion because the response to our action is out of our hands. That is the mystery of work, the mystery of love, the mystery of friendship, the mystery of community — they always involve waiting. And that is the mystery of Jesus' love. God reveals himself in Jesus as the one who waits for our response. Precisely in that waiting the intensity of God's love is revealed to us. If God forced us to love, we would not really be lovers.

All these insights into Jesus' passion were very important in the discussions with my friend. He realized that after much hard work he had to wait. He came to see that his vocation as a human being would be fulfilled not just in his actions but also in his passion. And together we began to understand that precisely in this waiting the glory of God is being revealed to us.

The Glory of God and Our New Life

Resurrection is not just life after death. First of all, it is the life that bursts forth in Jesus' passion, in his waiting. The story of Jesus' suffering reveals that the resurrection is breaking through even in the midst of the passion. A crowd led by Judas came to Gethsemane. "Then Jesus . . . came forward and said to them, 'Whom do you seek?' They answered him, 'Jesus of Nazareth.' Jesus said to them, 'I am he.' . . . When he said to them, 'I am he,' they drew back and fell to the ground. Again he asked them, 'Whom do you seek?' And they said, 'Jesus of Nazareth.' Jesus answered, 'I told you that I am he; so, if you seek me, let these men go' " (John 18:4–8, RSV).

Precisely when Jesus is being handed over into his passion, he manifests his glory. "Whom do you seek?...I am he" are words that echo all the way back to Moses and the burning bush: "I am the one. I am who I am" (see Exod. 3:1–6). In Gethsemane, the glory of God manifested itself, and they fell flat on the ground. Then Jesus was handed over. But already in the handing over we see the glory of God who hands himself over to us. God's glory revealed in Jesus embraces passion as well as resurrection.

"The Son of Man," Jesus says, "must be lifted up as Moses lifted up the serpent in the desert, so that everyone who believes may have eternal life in him" (John 3:14–15, JB). He is lifted up as a passive victim, so the cross is a sign of desolation. And he is lifted up in glory, so the cross becomes at the same time a sign of hope. Suddenly we realize that the glory of God, the divinity of God, bursts through in Jesus' passion precisely when he is most victimized. So new life becomes visible not only in the resurrection on the third day, but already in the passion, in the being handed over. Why? Because it is in the passion that the fullness of God's love shines through. It is a waiting love, a love that does not seek control.

*It is in the passion that
the fullness of God's love
shines through.
It is a waiting love,
a love that does not
seek control.*

When we allow ourselves to feel fully how we are being acted upon, we can come in touch with a new life that we were not even aware was there. This was the question my sick friend and I talked about constantly. Could he taste the new life in the midst of his passion? Could he see that in his being acted upon by the hospital staff he was already being prepared for a deeper love? It was a love that had been underneath all the action, but he had not tasted it fully. So together we began to see that in the midst of our suffering and passion, in the midst of our waiting, we can already experience the resurrection.

If we look at our world, how much are we really in control? Isn't our life in large part passion? The many ways in which we are acted upon by people, events, the culture in which we live, and many other factors beyond our control often leave little room for our own initiatives. This becomes especially clear when we notice how many people are handicapped, chronically ill, elderly, or restricted economically.

It seems that there are more and more people in our society who have less and less influence on the decisions that affect their own existence. Therefore it becomes increasingly important to recognize that the largest part of our existence involves waiting in the sense of being acted upon. But the life of Jesus tells us that not to be in control is part of the human condition. His vocation was fulfilled not just in action but also in passion, in waiting.

Imagine how important that message is for people in our world. If it is true that God in Jesus Christ is waiting for our response to divine love, then we can discover a whole new perspective on how to wait in life. We can learn to be obedient people who do not always try to go back to the action but who recognize the fulfillment of our deepest humanity in passion, in waiting. If we can do this, I am convinced that we will come in touch with the glory of God and our own new life. Then our service to others will include our helping them see the glory breaking through — not only where they are active but also where they are being acted

45

upon. And so the spirituality of waiting is not simply our waiting for God. It is also participating in God's own waiting for us and in that way coming to share in the deepest love, which is God's love.